GHOSTWORD

CRISOSTO
APACHE

Gnashing Teeth Publishing
242 E Main St
Norman AR 71960

Cover Artwork: "Unusual Specter" by Crisosto Apache

Cover Design: Gnashing Teeth Publishing

The cover font is A Asian Ninja and Ablation (Under License from
VP Creative Shop)

The interior font is Georgia

Printed in the United States of America.

ISBN: 979-8-9854833-3-8

A Gnashing Teeth Publishing First Edition

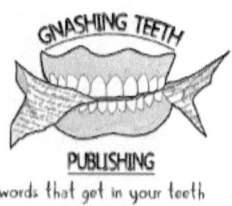

— for my spouse, Todd
the one meaning in my life

— & for my father, Alfred
who never stopped searching

Preface

Most journeys begin without knowledge of ever beginning. *Ghostword* is inspired by Ryunosuke Akutagawa's last manuscript and publication, *A Fool's Life* (1987, Eridanos Press), written on June 20, 1927. My introduction to Akutagawa's work by Arthur Sze helped facilitate the concept behind this body of work in 1990, while attending the Institute of American Indian Arts in Santa Fe, New Mexico. Unfamiliar with Akutagawa's work, I did not realize the profound influence his writing had on Japanese culture during his life and afterward. Akutagawa's writing influenced the Japanese filmmaker Akira Kurosawa, famously known for *Seven Samurai* (1954), who directed two films based on Akutagawa's stories, *The Grove* (1950) and *Rashōmon* (1950). Akutagawa's *A Fool's Life* is a written collection of fifty-one short what I call "poetic vignettes" after which my collection *Ghostword* is inspired and mimics, slightly, with some of the titles. The collection has three parts that conversate with each text.

Reading excerpts from Akutagawa's collection parallels some of the conflicted nature of erasure, which many of the vignettes exhibit; along with my conflicts of belonging as a gay Apache and Diné Native American, while growing up on the reservation and off the reservation. Carrying a carbon copy of the book with me for many years gave me time to reflect until I was finally challenged to respond. In the method, I read each numbered "poetic vignette" and chose sections that stood out. The beginning of the writing process was difficult because I tried to mimic the time frame in which Akutagawa wrote *A Fool's Life*. The reason being that Akautagawa's time frame for composing *A Fool's Life* corresponds with his act of suicide over approximately three hours. During the three hours, Akutagawa wrote what I call his "swan song." I was only able to respond to twenty-one sections of the fifty-one, which makes up the first section of this collection. A second three-hour attempt makes up the second section. Utilizing the time frame of Akutagawa's death was difficult and strange because of the issue of death and the taboo beliefs of

Apache & Diné culture. Also, some might see the process and utilization of a "death" time as morbid. Finally, in the third section, I responded to discussion-like resonances in some of Akutagawa's other narrative work.

In the body of work for the first draft, I had kept the numbered sequences but chose to eliminate them, to demonstrate consistency throughout the collection. Some poems have the same titles, and others have the same titles coupled with the Mescalero Apache language dialect. The Mescalero Apache language has been influential in my identity, and has historical significance, and adds to the disparities and dispositions that coincide with my existence growing up on the reservation and off. I have also chosen to accompany each poem with a quote from *A Fool's Life* and other Akutagawa texts to show the correlation inside the composition as a body of work responding to each entry. The inclusion is what solidifies the text as a collection. Later in the revision process, I added the numbers for each text back into the final draft to correlate with Akutagawa 's entries.

My attempts to correlate and link the Mescalero Apache language led to an inclusion of a note section clarifying any challenges in translation. A cycle of life experiences separates each section beginning with birth, then moving into adulthood, and then death transforming the collection into the next world, offering some relief for the influence of the composition and, also giving credence to not allowing Akutagawa's spirit to linger. The discovery of self or existence sometimes takes a lifetime to acknowledge, but the journey can be lasting. Sometimes, I am unsure of my experiential life outcomes. The textual and experiential connection is the concept I tried to establish in this collection, as I carried with me the carbon copy of Akutagawa's final manuscript all those years and as I finally obtained a physical copy of his book.

Crisosto Apache
March 2021

Table of Contents

A Life

I exist now in a most unhappy happiness. But strangely, without remorse. [...] In the manuscript, consciously at least, there is no attempt to justify myself. [...] At the fool in this manuscript, go ahead and laugh. – Ryunosuke Akutagawa 20 June 1927

1. The Pages

For a time, from the ladder's top, he had
been watching them. – R. Akutagawa, 1.
The Age

— now, more than twenty-five years ago
making my passage, a wandering made confining words
through a folded athenaeum, a dark place old as fingers,
turning the paper shells of overused lines on shelves

discovering more of those names, names calling
from beyond the mountains, from beyond the sea,
from beyond the madness, & disheveling confessions

repetition of tousled vowels led them into a deep lull
of flat slivers, smelling of mold and replete decay,
sifting through each repeating voice in a tenacious howl

Oh. the mountains of Han-Shan, Oh, the disobedience
of Milton, Oh, the insanity of Poe, and the many
woes of Plath, — each full of the sinking glares

— if I still feel small against them, then for that small moment
in my life, I can sense an inure stutter toward each word
of Anglo utterance, and forget I ever heard calling their names

leaning into them as twilight learns into its coming dread,
those names remain a decade blur of my pages,
a forsaken twilight, unlike my unfamed beginning, ik ł'dá

— my own half century's end is still undetermined

2. Shí ma / My Mother

Just a brick wall, the ledge planted with fragments of broken bottle. – R. Akutagawa, 2. Mother

in a sating ritual old as the polished grain on the pine vessel,
my mother leading me by my little fingers down the aisle
of each worn pew

on this very Sunday toward the front of each steady row,
she prefers to sit askew just so she can hear the droll organ blurt
the dull notes of some eager redemption
— so she thinks

and to hear the pathetic rotary sermon drooling from a vacant
whittling facial frame, whose eyes sift over every black shoulder

she tries to avoid the ocular slide at a differential pace from
the pastor's glance and the fracturing light emanating from
the colored windows that coat the outer ends of the congregation

this very Sunday fixating on the multi-color panels of stained glass,
away from the stench of dried pine, preserving skin, eyes, and teeth

this very Sunday a sick feeling took hold of me and the vessel
containing the origin of her own words searching for the white
orbs lost inside the soul turn up onto herself there in the front row
a resigning swathed word to a coffin, to the ears where she never
bid a formal farewell

3. Kúghą / Home

*In the outskirts in a room on the second
floor he slept and woke.* – R. Akutagawa,
3. Home

my boyhood home became periphery because of its location
eight miles away from town, the house I grew up in was now empty

burrows inside a thicket of forest left pockmarks on the hillside

inside the copse remained an empty cask, a remnant
     of my thick body
which has now become the shape of a log of rotten wood

— then, no one could hear
the arguments and screams, the echoes that reverberated through
the tree limbs and leaned against my inner ear becoming part
of the silhouetted tree line

outside along a small embankment next to the empty house where
I used to lie sideways with my head nearest the ground
— where I watched
the soldier beetles carelessly roam below the swaying parabola
of slumped sunflowers, where a tuft of sod imprints
     a smudge lasting

I returned to the vacant house occasionally to stand
on the embankment still imprinted in my facial skin, transfused

— then I think of the room
now my body, a rooted rotted waste of immersing follicles
against my hairline weaving the forgotten voices
and somnolent soil not forgetting the family line
which is my forest that forever becomes
— the outskirts of my home

5. Id

The words opened for him an unknown realm, —close to the gods, a realm of 'Self'. It was painful. And ecstatic. — R. Akutagawa, 5. Self

my cranial realm of woe is a realm of a kind of *self*,
standing toward a bathroom mirror, disguised
in some small hotel in the Midwest as the wind yowls
just outside the window   — in this realm through
the mirror sits a painful fleshy lump which
drapes over a yellow armchair

I look in the mirror at my own eyes staring back
and with every exhale stacks the smoke fumes
in a hazy dream erasing the lines of the fare
of assurances for what sits in the yellowish armchair

behind the smoke puffs my revelry and small
condoling embers record the unknown reddish words
but according to my written words and some wistful
jeremiad   — or better yet, the hollow cries near to ~~God~~,
I whisper empty to him
—I am not all that important

6. A Sickness

*Thinking up life's brevity, once more he
conjured up the blossom of the palm.* –
R. Akutagawa, 6. Sickness

in a guttural hesitation I scramble for an English dictionary,
much like a glottal stop I look up the following words,

ké bichį gúúlí'í: leather boots with a toe guard,
haada'ał: to sing forcibly,
tł'u łibáyí: medicinal blessing herb twelve inches to two feet tall,
greyish green color with a musty smell, similar to mildew
but sweeter, its potency is better when the leaves just sprout
— there is more to its scent than just being a plant,

in a quick hesitation I clamor to annunciate the stumbling sounds
but in my imagination, the words only come out as gibberish,

tightening my hands and my eyes roll back into my tongue,
to form the box shape and with my larynx, I loosen
the forgotten lingual lineage,

shaking the blackened voices from my sputum I also loosen
the flowing blood identity that enables me to connect my voice
to the body because I know now, and discover how blindly
I acknowledge the bloodshed involved

8. Fireworks

But those violet blossoms of fire, -- those
awesome fire works in the sky, to hold
them, he would give his life. — R.
Akutagawa, 8. Sparks

an ignition of colorful sparks blooms at dusk as I begin
the long night dance into dawn, scruples of tiny embers
are released and from the surging palms I grip the yucca
sword now used to shield and consecrate my movements,

the sparks ascend forming the decadent bouquets separating
form from the deepening indigo that collides with the stars,
at the edge of all widening ebb that I am pulled towards
the inevitable black sky hearing the hiss of twinkling ghosts
— long since burnt

upon midnight, the intermittent crackling bursts, and releases
a superficial haze as the distant detonations encumbers
the somber deadness of my conquered existence in a display
of dissolute coloration, the light surges and hides a type
of meaning   — I tuck away from my relatives
into the celebration meant only for those unlike me,
a celebration recognizing the awful American, ~~Fourth of July~~

9. Corpse

He stared at the body. — R. Akutagawa,
9. Cadaver

in my culture, there has always been a taboo about handling
the dead

one autumn afternoon walking down a dim slow hallway
passing many locked doors
— there is a hush
to the intermitting lights telling secrets lingering behind
each of those doors
— autumn waits outside the building
and carving me with a lurid stench of old plastic bags
— left out in the sun, too long

the room is downstairs, where she lays tucked away
in a grey soundless rectangular space
— she lays quieter than she is

a gaunt soundless toe-tagging shell of a woman, nothing
— but a small aiming frame

in that lightless room, she absorbs the cold table under
a twinge strobing light dissolving the blue clotting cloth
covering her
— the wedge in her chest cavity
whispers the surgical precision of passion gazing
at her suffocating fingertips
— a greyish bile color
an unwillingness in her dermis somehow means murder,
and validating the availability of consenting cadavers

10. Teachers

*In the autumn sunlight the oak stirring
not a slightest twig's leaf.* – R.
Akutagawa, 10. Mentor

hauling around these ligneous crates containing copies
of authors signed books, old manuscripts, and scraps
of paper along with my own rejected scriptures
that reveals the extensions of exerted tree branches
and connections to frail bridges over land masses
and the remaining voices of contained bodies of water

the stationary mentions semantic connections inside
each sheet of flattened pulp concealing all my belongings,
belongings I thought would make me a better writer

I can only remember the one tree and its branches ever reaching,
underneath each limb shadowing the letters, consonants
and vowels of where I am
— *awake* and still thumbing through
each page trying to figure out how I will carry each copy,
and each word inside those damp pages — the breeze gently
courses
— I remain wavered, unmoved, and dreaming

14. Union

*A bowl of yellow narcissus, her gift to
him, in front of her.* – R. Akutagawa, 14.
Marriage

— to start,
I was close to penniless and in debt, and he was the one
who was obliged to take me in, I a hopeless character
with a senseless backbone — the beginning few years
of our union, he carried me without cause or question

until the act of his financial embezzlement solidified
the lasting gift of doubt in our union, a union wasted
away on flecks of deteriorating yellow petals

— afterthought,
once the wilting yellow petals dropped, there they
remained in the jading years to come
— to see him in front of me

17. Moth

In wind reeking of duckweed, a
butterfly flashed. – R. Akutagawa, 17.
Butterfly

I somehow a noctuid maturing larvae
left flapping helplessly for a time
in a squall of blank wind still relentless
releasing the metallic feather dust
from my wings

many nights have come and gone
and I helplessly flutter nearby ferociously
and jutting against the bulb with each
passing nightly a pluming impact

each bombardment sends flecks of dust
discharging away from my plume-less body

at the final flicker, the light fades
and dawn emerges, a descending filament
flying outward in the approaching light,
coarsely settling on my rumpling cheek
— as bruises

18. Luna

*Following her with his eyes (they hadn't
even a nodding acquaintance) he felt a
loneliness such he'd never known... – R.
Akutagawa, 18. Moon*

my eyes will always wince against the bright
light because they cannot help it, the involuntary
reaction in the widening iris reacts uncontrollably
by the mind which will always determine its dilation

my skin on the other hand has difficulty
instilling its conformation to its moving actions
which will never avert a glare by errant light
forcing onto its constricting skin

— though
I have sat in the forgiving light many times,
the epidural attraction of living in *that* same Chiaroscuro
always leaves me in a seemingly self-containing loneliness

21. A Madness

Suddenly for her husband—for this husband incapable of securing her love, contempt. – R. Akutagawa, 21. Madwoman

— love
did not leave me, nor did it lead me

in a directional spiral of unanswerable situations
but the questionable shame from my stepfather's influence
did lead me to the following conclusions,

he who will remain an appalling frightened madman,

he who will only think of himself as old, deflated, & selfless,

he who will remain a fallible haunch & hollow form,

he who will live inside the lurid darkness of his bedroom,

he who will never know any other dissolving aspirations,

he who will be unremembered from these words written today,

he who will never hear the vowels or letters containing his name,

he who will not follow the ghosts and be unable to ascend,

he who will stink in the history of his effacing contempt,

he who will be the vessel of his corrosive jealousy,

he who will never have the time for and from a would-be son,

he who will always experience the tarnishing glimmer,

he who will wilt as a wavering whittled sliver,

and will be confined to a metal container

— a casket forever his home

23. He

*Side by side, they walked the dim
square. It was their first time together.*
— R. Akutagawa, 23. She

each year my caution in words persists,
as persistence in whispering words for poetry
— of reassurance

the words flout and we are untrustworthy
as night is to the blind and making
me wander relentlessly in our small house

the pacing hastens my pervasive pen
as I wait for him to effortlessly return

his return soon graces the page of dribbling ink,
the ink which unclogs the fingers from the arm

— maybe now
in these times of elating moments
we will nestle in our small square room
he will then whisper just before bedtime
into my ear, words securing the reassurance
— again,
like the time we first slept together

those elating words I have excitedly written
over and over has me welding myself this time
into the still whispers of my ear's slow delight,
— *there are no regrets*

26. Ghostword

Gazing up at them everything was forgotten. — R. Akutagawa, 26. Antiquity

the infinite ash of Łibáyí ascends with white skin,
these beings with misshapen faces rise from autumn
spark, and tussle their hand drums

their succinct song penetrates my ear and is suppose
to protect me from this sudden wide eye wakening
staunch, I glower beneath the stammering curative clutch
of the *mad man*, my damn stepfather

after years of emotional burial and systemic abuse
I escape only to unearth a museum of quality turmoil
which my family hid very well

after he causes my brother's death, I use my time
to carefully tuck away what is left of my brother's
belongings in a thicket of weeds behind my childhood
home, bound in a cotton cloth pouch I place the bundle
toward the east under a blue spruce tree

a ceremonial cluster of bags burning to ash within
the trusting palms of those misshapen beings of smoke
clasping, leaving my stepfather in a shameful glare,

— always lurking in the background

29. Torn

An iron wine bottle. — R. Akutagawa,
29. Form

sipping slowly from a delicate
crystal form, a stemmed glass
leaves me in a dizzying dither

inapt to speak coherently
for a night I learn to lean
from this glass and follow
in the footstep of my linage

in this perpetuate stupor,
I define a false sense
of my imminent self
and apart from my imminent
beauty I always shy away
from its sly form still deeming to me
a complicated full red glass

— turning yellow every time

30. Drizzle

Even to his self scrutinizing self the
answer came as surprise. — R.
Akutagawa, 30. Rain

in my mouth, I barely remember
laying on the front porch rail
young as drizzling rain begins

making those tiny clapping sounds
painfully hitting the arid ground
and always associating spring
luring inside me with an early spray

— asking himself
am I worthy of my written words,
or are my written words worthy of me?

I roll off the heavy rail
and stumble from the porch

from the obvious answer
I found the word on my forehead
and on my laden drunken breath
wheezing with compelling wetness

— always in my blood

34. Conquered

That seven or eight years ago he hadn't understood color, he realized now. — R. Akutagawa, 34. Color

— as I permanently expect
I unscrew the caps on each paint tube

I squeeze the first paint tube
releasing a bit of white titanium color

I then open the next paint tube
and squeeze the second color

I scoop a small bit of scarlet red
that seeps onto the unsettled pallet

I render the two colors together
and in time I add a bit more titanium
white creating an adulterate red

each time I mix in more white
and it dilutes the red even more

and each time I blend in more white
— I lose a greater part of myself

38. Vengeance

That the cruel urge was in him, he could not deny... — R. Akutagawa, 38. Revenge

I refuse to call him a *father*

no one will ever understand
the many compartments I call *home*

they just became sections that add
to the partitions of a house
maybe also our relationship

I only guess he did not know how
to be a father let alone how to recover as a man
— forgetting the human part

not having any biological sons I was one of three
who was a threat to his fatherly nature

one day I would mature and challenge his dominance

it eventually would happen as I have predicted
leaving one a drunk, one dead, and I
a lonesome wrought-out writer

— he and I never speak anymore

we tried mending our relationship but like mythology
it became supposed and unrealistic

since our failed attempt to reconcile a kind of kinship
I now only acknowledge a voiceless violence
— a stoic stalemate

41. Cardiac

But he knew the cause of his malady. —
R. Akutagawa, 41. Sickness

— the caution in starting a chainsaw

the buzzing vigor generates an onset
and eases the space between my ears

as the massive jolt from the metallic
melodic rigor rages from the chainsaw

what my *supposing father* does not know is
pulling on the trigger can cause a negative
interaction with his pacemaker

the space between my ears bows upward
plumping my cheeks and creasing crows
feet, almost in a hopeful snicker

a tiny thought in my head voices its concern
to warn my *supposing father*, leaving me with
this dismal decision to notify, but contrary
to my *supposing father's* heart condition is
— do I dare warn him not to cut wood?

— or should he die trying?

50. Confined

But to believe in a God, -- to believe in a
God's love, that was impossible. — R.
Akutagawa, 50. Captive

many of friends went astray as whispers away from the faith,
many of friends went astray from the faith as whispers, away

in the exhaust of these whispers, I become the air of arid fall
as it torments my hands of some presence, by some torment
— of a ~~God?~~

Here I pace inside my small square room in falls' remains
I persist the empty space, but the room inside is small & arid

inside I am small, and I believe the pace of this arid room inside
I stray from the belief of a falling whisper and this small room

belief in friends fail in the small space of this whisper
yet, in this whisper friends fail and may fall into an exhaust

I have paced the floor for so long and I have gotten better at it

but the arid belief in ~~God~~ fails the small spaces of this room
but mostly arid whispers pace the presence of small beliefs

— to believe in a ~~God~~, is to believe friends exist

51. Conquest

In this semi-darkness day to day he
lived. — R. Akutagawa, 51. Defeat

— inside a determining dark,
inside my condensing state of mind so much clarity to consider
inside my conflicting state of mind so much conjecture to clarify

as the sordid yellow lump of flesh draped over a yellow armchair
I presume defeat and control of a place that controls sad people

I presume to manifest the sadness that continues to exist and resist
I challenge daily the destiny which is my darkest hour of living

my inevitable state of succumbing is the dark ~~American~~ hour

an opinion like all options leaves nothing to clarify even after
a conclusion formed based on incomplete information

by use of force, or by use of this state of mind, the darkness
manifests a destiny left in a gripping palm and blank conjecture

nothing is determined, nothing determines the outcome without
a belief conjectures a consideration leaving no controlling belief
and yet outside the wind blows the dry leaves about

— the day continues to move on without me

A Death

The blade nicked, a slim sword for a stick. — Ryunosuke Akutagawa

4. Salt Well

In full bloom the blossoms in his eyes a
line of rags, sad. – R. Akutagawa, 4.
Tokyo

blooms of yucca and cactus blend together
in a greenish hue, these colors line the ledges
of my eye every time I walk past in the shadow
of dził guyzanni, my holy white mountain

beneath its peak, I graze the tops of buffalo grass
away from the pace of lines coursing through a path

my artery through the stretch of gravel roadway
streams through wildflowers

the weed stalks surge in a breeze just before dusk
as I limp along the trail wading through the gray

many times I tread through dirt roads remembering
the beat in hollow steps, the reaping heartbeat
and the grumbling stone against stone

through the grey, I see salvation in a honey-lit window,
in the distance reaching, just before the lost thicket tree line

I did not remember the walk from my grandmother's house
being this long, a deep lumber longing to embrace my torso

lost to this path, my legs linger hobbling as horses
do in the nearby pastures

— the walk was longer than I care to remember

7. Titivation

All at once he was struck. – R. Akutagawa, 7. Pointing

— standing before four of them
I dress in this worthless form as they march in place tapping
blades against their leather skirt

staying in a sturdy gaze through the depth of their smudged eyes

tiny tin cones jingle against each other as larger copper bells clank
they form a huddle by the oak brush arbor and others come to join

smearing ash upon each limb and lightning jags above each arm
surges the commencement of stars

spackles of black glistening through their torso inside white streaks
oscillate in my once open eye slits

etching worm & vertical scars lay upon my wrist as electric plumes
spreading inside my archaic stance

thwarting hide slams in a two-beat dance wiping a white line across
my nasal bridge carrying a benediction against a somnolent sky

with each crown, their arms vacillate in motion with an outward Y
releasing a shimmering body of dying celestial ghosts
— through some millennia

the metal noise ends my doubt, breaking my worthless vanity in two
carving away through my ghastly spray against Earth's atmosphere

summoning the creatures who now protect me
from the ever-red drip
from the worthless clay I am now dressed in

11. Dawn

In the sky exactly overhead glittered a
star. – R. Akutagawa, 11. Night's End

each morning I find myself facing east, spreading
an offering of pollen towards a grove of juniper trees

longing for an embrace maybe a veracious prayer

I place no plausible reason for my mistakes in the past

sixty-four winter cycles did not feel any colder to me

one early morning I remembered an overcoming color

I found myself in a vacant parking lot across the street
from where I used to live, sitting in my empty Chevrolet
pickup truck with my coat bundled under my head,
because I was locked out of the house again

the frigid air tries hard to separate me from my kids
but it brings them close into my longing embrace

I clutch the tuft of coat tighter under my head
trying to embrace a kind of security

A security that brings me close to the sight where
I witness a meteor shower spraying

— just above my beating heart

12. Carrizo
for E. Daklugie

> *The submarine's inside was dim.* – R.
> Akutagawa, 12. Naval Base

in my youth I hitched a ride to San Diego, across
chirping desert and distant night, I gazed upon a slow
moving dark encasing a convex cerulean cavity

each night I stood beneath the sky for hours mesmerized
at the perplex reformatory of twinkling lights and broken
glass fragments spreading against a glistening sunset

a faceless man behind a lost reflection of a glass
at a drive-up window informs me
too bad, you know nothing of your past

how far will I walk against the night
confirming to captivity I had never realized

some years later under the kitchen table they all huddle
as the rampage continues toward the back of the house

a clash of debris crashing from the other room recoils
and broken sounds escape the barricade of doors

***

— all I remember is returning in 1970

— all they remember is me sitting at the edge of my bed
with the war still in my hands

13. Posthumous

Sky bleak. — R. Akutagawa, 13. Mentor's Death

— nothing drags like the calm of a winter's night
— a train whistle resonates through the frost air
— religiously he stands outside smoking cigarettes
— he always has to blow smoke into the frigid air
— each exit of breath awaits a closer extinguishment
— the redbud of his cigarette brightens every time
— a vanquishing fear lumps inside my throat
— with each exhale I think to myself
— one day I will have to antagonize
— a fate of his inevitable demise
— meanwhile, I will endure
— driving a long highway
— remembering home
— each plume
— dissipates
— out the car
— window

15. Bungalow

They lived in peace. – R. Akutagawa, 15.
They

in the beginning, we always fought and argued
over little things, like how much time it took
to leave our house, or where the cups should
be placed in the cupboard, and how long we each
showered in the morning

then our apartment became a smaller one-bedroom

now I just hug him from behind hoping to recapture
a brief nature of our beginning

I will always remember the small one-bedroom
apartment with yellow walls where we shared
our first communion inside the twilight city
forging our way through a will that will always
leave an encapsulation of hope through our ramblings

16. Slumber

That even such a pillow might house a centaur, he didn't seem to realize. – R. Akutagawa, 16. Pillow

— in a dream
I remembered how to slay a sheep

a careful slit and more than a nick
leaves it more relaxed than before

I caress its velvet ear and whisper
empty blessings into the funnel
chasm waiting for its voice to mutter
back at me until it shutters and finally
stops moving

— in my waking dream I forget

in another sleep I clench a pillow tight
not knowing the clench against my neck

desperately sputtering and repeating
the dying words of my empty dream

Until one has loved an animal,
a part of one's soul remains unawakened.

— something Anatole France wrote

19. Flight

*Unfolding these man-made wings,
easily he glided up into the sky.* — R.
Akutagawa, 19. Man-made Wings

Eagle volunteers to carry
all my prayers
to the Sun,
as an equal
to a father
a deity, or a ~~god~~

on his ascent
he undergoes the dense
force of Sun's rays

Eagle returns to earth
with singed wings

in his reoccurring ascension,
Eagle finds himself
looking into the Sun

Eagle places his right wing
over his eyes,
blocking Sun's rays

although Sun warms
his feathers
Eagle can never
find himself
inside the rays
of its illumination
and never carrying
my undeserving prayers
— upward

20. Handcuffs

All the obligations were his. – R. Akutagawa, 20. Shackles

when I decided to take her
as a wife, it never occurred
to me that it would leave us
with several living obligations
— the kids

to which I would never oblige

now I care less about obligation
and stand shivering against a yellow
form still hanging on that armchair
— as a faulting memory

before the stain seeps in we were a circle
to each other leaving scars as ringed heirlooms
or saturate bracelets

these restraints will unwaveringly
pull at all your children
and *their* children's children

linking us all seamlessly and equivocally
to those historical bracelets
— unobligated

22. A Model

He discovered in the painter a poetry
unknown to anyone. – R. Akutagawa,
22. A Painter

a birthday card photograph illustrates
a pose alluring to any adolescent pansy boy

the card postures a tall slim well proportionate frame

harnessing a navy-blue tank top and a numeral stance

luring each of the boy's fingers with an enticingly lithe glance

like the silent ricochets of precise alliteration,
the model spoke a cortex language
laminating across the cardstock folds
encumbering the boy's fingers more

during an autumn walk, more like hitchhiking
the boy notices in a nearby thicket of lush brush

a small rabbit carcass reminding him
of the man inside the greeting card

later down the road the boy
saw himself in that carcass

— an unrelated postulate complication

24. Ts'ál / Cradle

And this was the wife's first baby. A
boy. — R. Akutagawa, 24. Childbirth

she panics and crouches inside the house
trying to barricade the doors from the pounding
but forgets they are locked from the outside

she clutches the yellow *cradleboard*
tight against her ribs

she tries to hush the terrified infant
she is afraid her husband has returned

this fear of not ever leaving
this fear of not knowing
and each time he returns it feels
like the end for them
— each time...

maybe one afternoon she will break away
and save her little boy
save him from his endless cry

his cry will forever hover inside
the yellow buckskin *cradleboard*

when the lock to the front door is forgotten
maybe, it will loosen the dusting color of pollen

maybe, the color will absolve them both one day

25. Name

*Standing in the doorway, in the
pomegranate blossoming moonlight. —*
R, Akutagawa,25. Strindberg

he sits inside a bar at a table

the smoke silhouette immerses
forming the name of his rapturous lie

the smoke seems to make out her outline
with seams of his fume as she pivots
sultrily in the corner against
the humming flickering lights

she slowly moves towards him

she will always find herself
inside the smoldering columns of lies

she is still separated inside his lie

she will never see herself
in that same light again

27. Predecessor

He, looking off to where the street
banged up against the spring hills, not
able to hold back. — R. Akutagawa, 27.
Spartan Discipline

I was walking down the street trying to remember
a history historians thought was worth recording

the memory was about a death of an ancestor
assumed drunk resulting in an ironic death in 1909

his death is later determined an accident

I read while he lived in the Blue Mountains,
this ancestor was peaceful maybe even passive
dying of natural causes, a heart attack on horseback
but historians claim he was drunk, and fell
off his horse breaking his neck, at the base
of a mesa near Casas Grande, Mexico
— this is the unforeseen irony about his life

one day I try to explain the story to a friend as he turns
to me and says, *it is only history, white man's history*

not recognizing the same pain in each of our lineages
which stems from the same governmental violence
and not thinking about the suffrages bestowed on our people
I reply, *not only history... but murder*

this conversation unfortunately remains ironic
and will continue to flourish from within

28. Murderer

for my mother & her mother

> *How long had he been repeating these words over and over In his head. Kill who?* — R. Akutagawa, 28. Murderer

Kúghą nągh kaą gú, díł'nán díndá!

the repetition of this phrase
fills her stomach with a reliable tightness

he repeats these words each time he gets drunk

one day, as a result, her daughter visits her in the hospital
— just before her death

When we get home, we are going to spill the blood!

31. Forced Migration

The house of his sister and his half-brother burnt to the ground... — R. Akutagawa, 31. Great Earthquake

from the one they called the *Dreamer*
his predictions were very clear

he sees the defeat of US soldiers
and the rise of his ancestors

— meanwhile
bullets zip in unpredictable patterns across
the desert canyons, and vitreous rock slabs

slugs lodge inside the earth, and sand

the aftermath left debris scattered leaving
brush arbors ablaze while his song echoes

after days in the heat, the bodies begin to bloat

hot in the sun babies cry among the brush
children wander as others cling to motionless mothers

weapons in hand the smoke billows

they are almost killed off
they dwindle to a handful
they are packed tight into stock rail cars
and ship forcibly east

— despite it all, they remain

32. Iłdá jiin'nájé'ká /Dance

*Locked in a struggle, they stumbled off
the porch.* — R. Akutagawa, 32. Conflict

stepson and stepfather embrace
in a violent *dance*, each pit himself against
the other and out of spite
their stagnant state for dominance escalates

this bone rage leaves them both tireless,
and both fetter in the untimely recognition
of blood sprawling against the door frame

Castilleja miniatas still grow under the loaded tree line

— the Indian paintbrush
painting the outskirts of meadow in vermillion blooms

33. Protagonist

Up on the icy summit not even the shadow of a condor could be seen. — R. Akutagawa, 33. Hero

négo'isdzanatł'eesh—white painted woman
naayé'nskąne—kills for earth
túbá'jish'diné—born in water
haastįń—first man

first man gazes long toward the mountain top
with no possibility of speaking up to them

twisted among the snowcap peak a woman covered
in white paste hangs alongside her two sons
one son stained with the blood of the earth
the other son dripping of thunderstorms

some days first man rushes up the mountain side
never reaching the top
other days he never emerges

but the moon still rises in cycles,
                        — for ceremony
and the rain still falls in cycles,
                        — for ceremony
the sun still shines in cycles,
                        — for ceremony
our life still begins in cycles,
                        — for ceremony
death still precedes in cycles,
                        — for ceremony
lest they forgive and despite the efforts of first man

he tries not to forget the cycle of ceremony

35. Lifeguard

Not a care when he died, to live a life of
intensity was his desire. — R.
Akutagawa, 35. Manikin

the boy tries to ignore his odious sentiment
toward his stepfather

the boy tries to keep his mind wandering

the boy watches the iridescent swimmers
at the town pool while sitting beneath tall pines

the lifeguard notices the boy staring
a quick twinge of shame
and another quick flinch
results in a slide of his eye

the boy continues to secretly study the lifeguard's
moving form

realizing how much the boy wants to be nearer
his thoughtless shame already makes up its mind

36. Meander

The fiery mountain aroused in him an
envy. But just why he couldn't say...—
R. Akutagawa, 36. Tedium

this man walks through a thicket of arduous brush
encountering a timid man he had never met before
they stood facing each other below a small rock cliff

one of the men says
I have never done anything like this before, have you?

the other says
uh, a few times I guess...why?

the first man responds
I suppose...it doesn't matter where you do it.

the first man makes up his mind about the timid man's
sour demeanor and figures they would never meet again

they depart with the first man relaying
I do not think we will meet again.

the timid man does not answer back and continues walking

streams of sexual denial will carry both men
and will quickly cease as hardening lava...

37. Northerner

It was painful, like watching frosted glittering snow drop from a tree's trunk. — R. Akutagawa, 37. The Northerner

his father comes from a northern region of Mexico

his father meets a woman whose brothers intervene

having no region to return he eludes to a violent end

there are miles of acreage on a reservation to bury
a man who is not wanted much like locating the first
sprouting spring shoot

a decaying smell will go undetected by any human nostril
yet is detected   by a vulture's hunger

40. Church Hoppers

You attack the present social system,
why? — R. Akutagawa, 40. Catechism

We are going to one of the other churches,
because this one is not teaching us anything.

they are divided into six religious denominations
and every Sunday they are missed by at least one

this is the irony that dodges their spirituality

among the already christened and less fortunate
they want to believe

42. Laughter

These words of two, three years ago returned. — R. Akutagawa, 42. Laughter of the Gods

one day, Coyote sees Duck walking her ducklings,
Coyote asks her how she keeps them in a straight line,
Duck says, she sews them together
with white horse tail hair every morning
and tugs on the line gently,
until the horsehair disappears,
that is how she keeps her ducklings in a row

as usual, Coyote leaves smiling, she sees a white horse
grazing in a nearby field,
she plucks a few strands of tail hair,
and returns to her burrow

the next morning, one by one
she begins to sew her pups together

when she finishes, she gently tugs on the horsehair,
and drags their little bodies along the ground,
Coyote tilts her head in dismay and becomes distraught,
she realizes she has killed her little pups

"Indians" will laugh about anything and anyone,
no matter the tragedy

43. Another Night

The wild sea in the dim light incessantly erupting in spray. — R. Akutagawa, 43. Night

evening comes with the sordid colors
of red & blue light, as ghosts harboring
among trees in a scathed darkness revealing
the tree trunk surface with every flicker

she stands on the porch again
with tears in her eyes not from sadness
or happiness but from the welts forming

she compresses the little hands and whispers
un-apologetic words and again explains
to the pouting children

"you see that bound man there... in the car?"

"...uh, huh"

"haastįń'dun'zhųdá'ná"

— he is broken

44. Death
for E. P. Botella/Kazhe

> *The dread, however, was not of death's*
> *agonies.* — R. Akutagawa, 44. Death

it is prohibited to whisper the names of the dead
as it encourages them to linger at the doorstep
and she has already lingered, far too long

45. Jewel Box

Born a eunuch. — R. Akutagawa, 45.
The Divan

when my mother was away
and my brothers were outside
playing with cousins
I would break into my mother's room
and fumble for her jewel box

I just could not help myself

I would begin the quick squirrelly ritual
adorning myself in shells, silver, and turquoise
desperately trying to recognize the person
staring back at me in the large dresser mirror

46. Lies

A tree rotting from the top down. — R. Akutagawa, 46. Lies

the absence of his biological father
pushes him toward criminal behavior

his mother did not defend the criminal
actions in a nontribal court

she will spend countless hours inside
the adult tribal court system trying
to justify more reasons for her husband
not to be incarcerated

it isn't until he reads *Genet* that he gleans
justification in his unnatural behavior
and continues his criminal behavior

in his pellucid dreams he envisions
his imprisonment as a vain criminal
who continually seeks a determined
sainthood

47. Fire

It was like the light of morning sun on thin ice. — R. Akutagawa, 47. Fire-play

dances flash against the dark swaggering sky

warm setting stars are comforting as flames crackle

resonance breeze heaves his beating heart

as the reverb ripples against his skin against the blazes

he will always marvel at his bubbling scorched skin

as part of the memory embedded beneath each scar

48. Second Death

He did not die with her. — R.
Akutagawa, 48. Death

she still whispers her mother's name, in private
hoping she can reconcile those absent days
what she will fail to realize, those days remain absent

49. Lamb

In front of him was neither madness nor suicide. — R. Akutagawa, 49. Stuffed Swan

this work is a sort of autobiography, a *poetic truth*

now that I think about that truth it is harder
to confront the transitions and oppositions in life

hearing once in a conversation the commonality
in all living beings was the color of their blood

staring, once into the eyes of a hanging lamb carcass
one summer and in that youth, blood began to drip
from a tiny pencil hole considered a dominant wound

there still are no tears only a disparaging realization
toward my life with complete humility always realizing
in front of him is neither death nor murder but a fate

— determined away from the flock

A Resurrection

For these words alone I would like to pardon his crime. —
Ryunosuke Akutagawa, *In a Grove*

Unwritten Letter

That instantaneous look of my husband,
who couldn't speak a word, told me all
his heart. — R. Akutagawa, *In A Grove*

existing inside my house; caressing my cold skin with oil
mimicking circular motions which lure your eyes away

a tickling wind attracts the concentrated sin in your fingers
parting a tuft of my hair and laying a strand of vibrant coral

existing inside my house in a mirror revealing my supple parts

time and time again fearing the act of contact hindering
your attraction toward my lissome skin, my brush stroke
holds more promise, my exposure to your sexual contempt

existing inside my house while you drive away in a glow
of red-light cinders, the light diminishing from the window
and move effortlessly towards reoccurring night when
waiting beneath the weight of the ceiling for your return.

existing inside my house where the lineup remains the same
like tiny medicinal soldiers in a row inside each burden bottle
of undeliverable messages descending the cabinet castle wall
dissolving a handful to clear my identity for my parts undefining

existing inside my hollow house as the warm water runs cold
and the suds lose their comfort swell, I will delay the notion
to dry my remains as the savior shaving blade falls making
no sound toward a flighty moth desperately clamoring to the light

— meanwhile, the slit always awaits

Fold

A dog, constantly teased, will not
rapidly jump at a piece of meat thrown
to him once in a while. — R. Akutagawa,
Yam Gruel

like that hanging lamb, trying to find peace inside,
as you move in greater numbers, through
the arroyos, you turn like a flock of birds
undulating in flight, upon arrival, and upon entry
you gather towards the far end of the corral
as you always have done

like that hanging lamb, trying to find peace inside,
where there are no fine wools or beds of brush,
only a time which shapes endless crests & plateaus,
a safe place to curl when night falls

like that hanging lamb, trying to find peace inside,
from a slight incision, it is time for your life to flow,
down your neck to the small violet pools below,
you will keep me alive if you are well prepared
with the care of skins, internal organs, and a range of meats,
each signifying a purpose to partake

like that hanging lamb, trying to find peace inside,
with this blade in hand, I feel the quick quiver
of your final sigh as you enter in and become
part of me, I must now acknowledge & understand
this burden when one day I must commit this violent
act but in turn, you will save the life, which is mine

Whitetail
for E. P. Botella / Kazhe

> *Beyond this was only darkness*
> *...unknowing and unknown.* — R.
> Akutagawa, *Rashōmon*

tree limbs and grasses move approximately
with the same circle sway and swooshing wind

they whisper among each blade and manage
to hold secrets, muddle behind loose walls
longing for open windows

the school bus makes its final stop in Whitetail
a mile down from my mother's house, I walk alongside
the road listening to gravel cracking beneath my step
and echoes above the tree line, pines emit their scent
and release a pollen drift intersecting with the spring air
and settles deliberate on my shoulders

from the roadway I approach the house
silent in the absence of my mother, house is empty
like the adjacent meadows which muffles my solitude

sunset gives way to the golden yellow outburst

above the tree line the house settles in the shadow
as I light the match the lantern exudes kerosene
I sit and wait listening to the beat of my heart
as it syncopates with the cricket songs outside

through the window the light dims to a slumber of slow grey
as I shuffle my feet to anticipate her arrival, silence intensifies
and lends itself to the settling frame of old angles of the house

the smell of sulfur and the flicker of my eyes
and plan to make my way to my aunt Nita's house

Witness

For the sublimity of life culminates in the most precious moments of inspiration. — R. Akutagawa, *The Martyr*

they say, *there are many kinds of terrible people*
they say, *there are many kinds of tasty people*

there are so many types of people who appear to be
— who stare for reasons unknown

in their unnatural manners or pretending personas
a kind of fictional struts in all direction particularly so

those smoky eyes supple lips and svelte hands
coupling with old fashioned curls in hairstyles
and a licking twist finishes their frontal appeal

the regard beneath their inner delicate ware
draws the eye away from what nurtures there
there are many types of people who appear

a curious nature of married people who recommend
an interesting grope or grasp and proceed to stare
at the inquisitive affair between the appearance of people
who recommend the pretense of indulging a persona
of this kind of pretend

if the curiosity persists and stirs beneath an attire
the truth of this desire and gaze upon the appearance
of these varying personas of people who are flitting
so elegantly across the floor

how do people come to avoid these bodies so unnatural
sly in appearance and has a choice to finish what has already
been achieved about the definition of people or the people
who appear to be another
— there are just so many types

Sapling

The human mind is in the dark.
With not a light to shine upon.
It burns a fire of worldly cares
To go and fade in but a span. — R.
Akutagawa, *Kesa and Morito;* "Morito's
Monologue"

I must say
this sapling
frail and green
stands aloof beside
the fence
on the west
side of the lot

when the first
snow falls
it covers
its top
and with its weight
begins to stoop

the bough so close
to the ground
and the leaves crinkle
with a finished season
long to unite
the sapling into
a lonesome horn

it remains all alone
in its place

Sleep
for my father Alfred

> *But as long as there was darkness, he*
> *believed in light that went with it. —* R.
> Akutagawa, *Cogwheels*; 5. Shakko

in sleep, summer dawns a shift
from slumbering eyes struggling
to open trying to remain joined with us

distant birds bicker above roadways
where awes of emergency vehicle shrill
against the drying dark igneous mesas

there is a dream and a time for resting
on a long hillside where his bed opens
to a widespread meadow under the overpass

irreversible... he sighs... *gone are my ills*

above the cranes fly away from benevolence

specks of rain begin to splash gallantly inside
the elegant cupping plumes of wet deer weed

from afar the light fights to enter the eyelets
as a forgotten word drifts out and unwritten

Casualties

*But now, how much better it is to die
even an ignominious death, than to live.*
— R. Akutagawa, *Kesa and Morito;*
"Kesa's Monologue"

white swab gauze
and red splotches
make the world
go around
pending the wound
that binds them

Poetic Thief

He would be brought to this gate and
thrown away like a stray dog. — R.
Akutagawa, *Rashōmon*

thievery perpetuates
the reasons for unoriginal work

stealing is next to godliness
— guilty
everyone is guilty

every print and word
has already been written

an allusion is the cloak of thieves
for which paper houses are built

Unfolding

When my breast grew cold, everything was as silent as the dead in their graves. What profound silence! — R. Akutagawa, *In A Grove*; 'The Story of the Murdered Man, as Told through a Medium"

*

love is trite and needs reinvention
touch only happens if we writhe in pain
sex sells itself and is only empty banging
and defines every aspect of our actual existence
rape exists because we don't look out for each other
as offense is the new courtesy

**

women and creation are still sacred
men and junk are a pointless concept
gender is expressed within us all
which include those not included
gays, homosexuals, and faggots need a new revolution
lesbians and dykes need to lead this uprising
HIV & AIDS are not a social disease, nor a memory lost on many
only a calamity for those who unknowingly become infected
— this is the only crisis

***

diagnosis is a scam and prescriptions
silence the masses into lacking choice
medication prolongs the inevitable
and nulls the contents inside our skulls
drugs are out of fashion because of prescriptions
alcohol should be given away hourly
because it is ineffective prescription against choice

****

birth leaves us all vulnerable
without adults we would wither
childhood remembers sexuality
and sometimes the abuse, but often forgets laughter
adulthood is built on seduction
and preys on the availability of the susceptible ones
old age is locked away in an infinite convalescence
and neglected to die, rot, and decay
— which is an easier suit to wear

*****

home is where a family congregates
but is often lost to financial institutions
a shelter is for those who cannot attain a home
homeless is a result of senseless invasions,
genocide, and displacement

******

peace does not exist
war is based on legal fiction
a purpose is undefined because
we still wander the earth senselessly

****

our blood color does not discriminate
race is categorized to settle apathy
ethnicity creates segregation for regulation
inside an edifice of boxes,
loss of identity is loss of soul
and self but not defined as a disaster,
names are kept warding off educated imbeciles

****
belief is the possibility
where many can exist
religion is the other scam
spirituality can determine a course
into the interior and exterior cosmos

artifacts remain unearthed to remind us of our existence

[*]
I am still solving for x

End Notes
The translations of text, which are not obvious, are translations in the Mescalero Apache dialect.

Page 2
Bí ma – translates to 'your mother'.

Page 4
Kúghą – translates to 'home' or 'house'.

Page 15
Łibáyí – is a deity in the Apache cultural tradition, last in a line of the four successive deities (also references the grayish color)

Page 24
Salt-well is one of many place names on the Mescalero Apache reservation.
Dził guyzanni – one of the four sacred Mescalero Apache mountains (East). Also known as Sierra Blanca

Page 27
Carrizo is a place name on the Mescalero Apache reservation.

Page 41
Ts ał – is a traditional cradle for an infant.

Page 39
Iłdá jiin'nájé'ká – is a traditional Mescalero Apache 'back and forth' social dance.

Page 46
haastįń'dun'zhų dá'ná – translates to "that man is not right, (a criminal)".

Page 56
Whitetail is a place names on the Mescalero Apache reservation.

Acknowledgments

Grateful acknowledgments are made by the author to the following: always to my mother Evangelina G. Apache; Alfred L. Platero, in memory of my father for reconnecting; Todd Andreff, my spouse, Arthur Sze for the introduction to a great writer Akutagawa Ryunosuke, and Luis Fernando Gomez for being such a great sport & photo subject for the cover; those who are my writing motivation and inspiration; James Thomas Steven, Allison Hedge Coke, and Chip Livingston for the reading of this work; Sandra Doe, an always respected mentor, teacher and elder; Reneé Ruderman for encouragement of structure and words for this collection; Judy Wilson and the editors of Yellow Medicine Review, Quincy Troupe, Heid E. Erdrich, Andrea Watson and editors of 3: Taos Press, the Poetry Foundation editors, editors of MetroSphere Literary Magazine, Jason Arment, Steven Dunn and the Denver's Veterans Writing Workshop, Ravi Kopra for the Hindi/Urdu translation, d.g. nanouk okpik, Tanaya Winder, Matthew Hohner and the crew at Loch Raven Review, Meca'Ayo Cole, Tara Shea Burke, Millissa Kingbird, Georgie Van Gunten, Joseph Jeffery, Leela Marlene Charley, Abigail Chabitnoy, tanner menard, Julian Talamantez Brolaski, Ericka Wurth, Hillary Leftwich, Margo Tamez, for my brothers, sisters, nieces, nephews and family.

Variation of these poems have been featured in the following:

MetroSphere: Casualties

Yellow Medicine Review: 43. Another Night (prior title, Captive), 50. Confined, 32. Iłdá jin'nágé'ká / The Dance, 46. Lies, 28. Murderer

Black Renaissance Noire: Unwritten Letter (prior title, A Letter Yet Written), Whitetail (prior title, House In Whitetail), Fold (prior title, The Fold), Unfolding (prior title, Unfolding [for Palatability])

All the Sins: 34. Conquered

POETRY Magazine: 12. Carrizo, 42. Laughter, 44. Death, 3. Kúghą / Home

Natural History Museum of Utah-Poetry Path (excerpt): 42. Laughter

Pearson, Inc (reprint): 42. Laughter

Loch Raven Review: 6. A Sickness, 9. Corpse, 38. Vengeance

The Rumpus: 8. Fireworks, 4. Salt Well

ANMLY Magazine: # 30 - Queer Indigenous Poetics: 41. Cardiac, 50. Confined (revised), 51. Conquest

Digging Through The Fat: 10. Teachers

Earth Song: A Nature Poem Experience (anthologized): 12. Carrizo

McGraw Hill Education(curriculum): 12. Carrizo

Bio

Crisosto Apache is originally from Mescalero, New Mexico (US), on the Mescalero Apache Reservation, and currently lives in the Denver metro area in Colorado, with their spouse. They are Mescalero Apache, Chiricahua Apache, and Diné (Navajo) of the 'Áshįįhí (Salt Clan) born for the Kinyaa'áanii (Towering House Clan) and are Assistant Professor of English. They hold an MFA from the Institute of American Indian Arts in Santa Fe, New Mexico. They are also the Associate Poetry Editor for *The Offing* Magazine. Crisosto's debut collection is ~~GENESIS~~ (Lost Alphabet, 2018).

FURTHER REFLECTION ON
ON
GHOSTWORD
BY
TIFFANY WOODLEY

1.   Ghostword is inspired by a collection by Ryunosuke Akutagawa called *A Fool's Life*. Think about the connotations of the two titles. What role does these titles play in the context of the work as a whole?

2.   In the first section of the collection, there are a number of poems which slip between reality and a more surreal experience such as in "A Sickness" and "Vengeance." How do moments of un-reality help to clarify the emotional subtext?

3.   A number of poems wrestle with the speaker's relationship with America and Americana, including "Fireworks", "The Pages" and "Conquered." What tensions exist between the speaker and America? What is the message those tensions help to define?

4.   Apache often uses dashed lines to conclude poems. At times, this creates a concluding statement while in others the line leaves the reader to draw their own conclusions. Check out some of the endings which do this, like in "Union" and "Handcuffs". Where does the ending send you?

5.   The second and third sections lean heavily into vivid visual and auditory imagery, mentioning "a slow / moving dark encasing a convex cerulean cavity"; "gravel cracking beneath my step / and echoes above the tree line"; and "blood sprawling against the door frame". Select an image that drew you into a scene. How did it affect your understanding of the poem?

6.   Yellow is an important color in Mescalero Apache culture. Its significance is tied to the role of corn pollen which is held sacred and connected to ceremonial traditions as a means of anointment. Look to times when yellow is a key color; given its significance, how does Apache's use of the color alter or develop your understanding of the piece?

7.   In "Poetic Thief", Apache writes, "stealing is next to godliness." Each poem is paired with an epigraph taken from Ryunosuke Akutagawa's works. What "stolen" lines were the most striking? In what ways do these lines interact with the poems they pair with?

8.   Separation and subsequent isolation is a recurring concept in these poems. Where does the author delve most deeply into emotions tied to otherness stemming from cultural practices, LGBTQIA identity, and familial seclusion?

9.   "Flight", "Titivation", and "Protagonist" each work to unpack failed attempts at connection and action which develop a sense of futility in the effort. What is the author's purpose in his inclusion of these moments?

10.   Throughout the collection, the speaker refers to a traumatic relationship with their step-father. Their mother is also a primary character and influence. How do these two relationships create contrast in the text? What emotions are tied to the stepfather? the mother? What is the relationship like between the speaker and his mother?

11.   There are a number of poems which stand out structurally including "A Madness", "Posthumous" and "Unfolding". What does the structure elevate or help to clarify?

12.   Throughout the collection, Crisosto Apache highlights past experiences that shape and refine one's identity. How do these poems work to both acknowledge the past and use personal history to build meaning in the present?

Other Volumes from Gnashing Teeth Publishing

Heat the Grease, We're Frying Up Some Poetry anthology

Love Notes You'll Never Read anthology

Winter limited release zine

Rain Minnows [Notecards and Poems] by Joshua Bridgwater Hamilton

Insurrection anthology

SHE: Seen. Heard. Engaged. youth anthology

Meditations & Mediations by Dr. Rebecah Hall

places I never want to see again by Keriann Gilson

Sleep Cinematic: A Golem's Quartet by Les Epstein

Lunafly by Raymond Luczak

Stepping on Legos limited release zine

When I Wear Bob Kaufman's Eyes by Tom Murphy

Forthcoming

La Santa Madre Tamalera by Juan Manuel Perez

You can purchase our books at http://gnashingteethpublishing.com

www.ingramcontent.com/pod-product-compliance
Lightning Source LLC
Chambersburg PA
CBHW021223260626
47172CB00002B/570